# Self-Proclaimed

A Novella by

William L.G. Stephens

Order this book online at www.trafford.com
or email orders@trafford.com

Most Trafford titles are also available at major online book retailers.

Printed in the United States of America.

ISBN: 978-1-4669-7001-4 (sc)
ISBN: 978-1-4669-7002-1 (e)

*Trafford rev. 11/16/2012*

 www.trafford.com

North America & international
toll-free: 1 888 232 4444 (USA & Canada)
phone: 250 383 6864 ♦ fax: 812 355 4082

# Dedication

I would like to thank "Modest Mouse", "Neutral Milk Hotel", "Brand New", and "Radiohead" for their incredible lyricism which has influenced me over the years. As well as the few friends and family that has stuck by me through my struggle with the world. Last but not least I would like to thank Danielle, without her *"Self-Proclaimed"* would not be readable. I would also like to thank my mother Rebecca Salvati, my sister Ericka Sebastian and Jennifer Trey for literally saving my life on four separate occasions, Little Jaida, Sgt. Yacezko, Pvt. Stroup, and Dr. Harrelson Klonopin.

# Contents

# Prologue

It was a little before midnight on a Friday. I was in a crowded basement with about twenty people. Metal music was blaring in the background. Hard alcohol was being passed all around by the bottle. Half naked women were dancing on the couches and boxes stacked up by the walls.

I lit a cigarette and sat back in a chair while I let someone I had just met tattoo an astronaut on the center of my chest. Two nights before I had seen the Australian astronaut Felix Baumgartner free fall twenty miles from the stratosphere, a jump which was fully paid for by Red Bull and had been two years in the making. The jump inspired me; it described how I felt, alone in outer space.

Though he was hardly an artist, the tattoo was looking like it was being done by a professional. The guy was only charging me seventy bucks. When the needle got to my sternum I quickly motioned over for a swig of some whiskey. One of the half-naked girls, barely over eighteen came by and poured the booze down my mouth. The booze spilt all over my eyes and up my nose, the girl was barely able to stand.

This little get together had been going on since around 8 p.m. Some of the people there weren't even in our graduating class, but they all had connections to dealers, or were old enough to buy liquor for the party.

The house was way out in the sticks, there wasn't another neighbor for about half a mile, and he was at the party anyways. So noise complaints were not an issue.

The city of Corona itself was run by the younger youth at night, we easily outnumbered the elderly. The city council meetings were nothing more than a joke. The parents that were involved in the meetings were the same parents that were letting their underage kids stay out late at night and get shitfaced.

I couldn't name one classmate that didn't drink liquor or didn't smoke marijuana. Those were the only two things to do in the city. You either joined the majority or stood out as an outcast.

I looked down at my chest; I was bleeding pretty heavily, due to the amount of alcohol in my blood. I had been drinking way before the party in the basement even began. I couldn't remember how I got to the home, but someone had told me my truck was parked outside in the grass, and I had knocked over a wooden fence. Mickey, the guy's house that we were at, could care less.

I wasn't the most social person in the room, but I had my own circle of friends, and talked to just about everyone at least once before. You couldn't avoid anyone in the city, no matter how hard you tried. Everyone knew everyone's business and that's just how things went.

One of the girls walked over to me and was checking out my tattoo. I had my eye on her for quite some time; she was the most attractive one at the party. Mickey had told me she wasn't running with anyone as far as he knew.

"It looks good." The girl couldn't help but smile when she saw me.

She had a nice body, c sized breasts, long legs, and judging by how many piercings she had in her ears and eyebrows I could only imagine where else she had them.

"I heard you were looking for someone to get a certain package off your chest."

I took a hit of my cigarette and exhaled.

"I was looking for a trade."

The girl reached down inside her bra and pulled out a piece of paper, she placed the paper in my hand.

"Call this number, and you'll get what you're looking for."

I looked down at the piece of paper; there were two different sets of numbers.

"What's the second number?"

The girl leaned down and kissed me. She then whispered in my ear. "The second number is mine."

I watched the girl turn around and walk back to her girlfriends. Mickey came by and sat down on a cooler right beside me.

"I told you I would hook you up."

I didn't normally challenge Mickey's word, but for this particular situation I had too.

"Are you sure he's reliable."

Mickey shook his head and took a drink of his beer.

"Absolutely I wouldn't drive you into a hole, you know that."

The package that the girl and Mickey were referring to was a large amount of Meth that I had received as payment instead of money. I had no interest in using meth, or dealing it. But it was either except payment or have nothing at all. For the past few weeks I had been looking for a buyer to get rid of the burden, but kept running into dead ends.

It was difficult to make a deal with someone I had never met before. But the way I saw it, Mickey didn't have any reason to burn me. Me and him had gone back a long ways, since childhood even.

I remained in the chair for another hour till my tattoo was finished. Once it was, I took a look in the mirror; it had come out a lot better than I had thought. I went to put my shirt back on, but the girl came by and took it out of my hands.

"Keep it off."

She threw my shirt on the ground and picked up a bottle of Tequila.

"When I drink tequila I tend to act a bit wild, that's ok with you isn't it?"

"Feel however you want around me. I don't judge."

The girl smiled.

"Thanks for the heads up."

She put her arms around my neck, and pushed her body up against me.

"So what's this guy's name?"

"He's a good friend of mine, people call him Rambo."

Rambo, what an odd nickname, I could honestly say I have never heard of him. But he may very well be the only connection in the area. I made it a point to call him later that night.

The events that took place that morning panned out in almost the same order that Rambo had explained to me.

My heart rate began to lower and my surroundings became clearer. Placing my hands upon my ribs I realized I had, without a doubt, broken them. I knew I should have sought medical attention, but I wasn't ready to answer the thousand questions that would go with it.

Three days had passed by and I hadn't mentioned one word to the police, or to anybody for that matter. If I told them now, they would want to know why I waited three days. And any excuse I would have given them would give them reason to believe I was somehow involved. The last thing I needed was to be a suspect in a murder case.

I confessed to no one what I had seen; I managed to eliminate some of the stress by writing in a private document on my laptop. When I wrote about it, I used made up names and formatted it like it was a screenplay instead of a witness report. I made certain that there wasn't one single detail that could be inferred as something that had actually happened.

# Chapter II

## Photogenic

I sat in my car with the radio on low and the engine still going. I was parked outside the market strip off of Del Rio in the upper scale part of Rancho Santa Margarita on a late Friday night. The stores were getting ready to close and the customers were all checking out. I was looking for a certain female in particular, one of whom I've known since my freshman year in High school and now a year after my graduation.

This female, who was newly nineteen and only a couple months older than me, was going to some cheap community college when she could be going to Cal State for some high speed degree in which the majority of the population of the world would have no interest. She was a beautiful photographer; I had spent many of my nights over at her one bedroom studio apartment, taking a close look at the photos she hung in her Dark Room. I would provide stories for these photos, as I had spent my entire senior year invested in Journalism with no real ambition to go any further with it than a High school credit.

The two of us connected on a different level of intimacy than most couples. Or, as she often likes to throw in my face, we used to connect. It's been only three months since she called it quits and no longer wanted to have any sort of relationship, which was clearly the right choice. Not to say I wanted us to end, but I'd rather not have her in my life at all then have her as only a friend. The connection that I speak of is in itself indescribable to anyone besides the two of us. But I figure by the way she went about moving on, she may not understand as well as I thought. Either that, or not have as strong of a connection as I thought we had in the first place. However, notably everything was on a different keel than it was in the early beginning.

This girls name was Sofia, Sofia Mertzon. A name I could never get out of my childish brain nor an elderly mind.

As I sat in my car I twiddled a letter back and forth in my hand like it would somehow disappear after time. The seal on the letter wasn't broken; I didn't have the balls per say to open it, in fear of what the context of the letter contained. I didn't have to open it to already know that it wasn't something heartfelt, that it wasn't something I'd want to hear. I knew behind the envelope were words that were just going to further push me in the direction I was headed, the direction of being practically unsociable and unintellectual to the rest of my friends, to the rest of my family, to the rest of society, and mostly to myself.

I no longer trusted my judgment or my choices over critical decisions, and once you get to that point of seclusion it's harder than a mother fucker to come back.

My name is Ollie Magnum and I' am not photogenic . . . but she is.

Off of Main St. and behind the Villas Antonio Apartments, there is a lake called "Time". At one period in the past I remember having Sofia's and my picture taken by a random person who didn't seem like they had anything better to be doing. Sofia, being a photographer, spent several minutes trying to pick an articulate person to capture the mood just right. Then she stated that there was no one who could do that as well as her and allowed me to choose the photographer.

In the picture I have my arm wrapped around her with an expression on my face I forgot I could make. After all the events since we split, I really can't tell if she was ever faking her smiles or her happiness, but in this picture she was smiling. I like to believe she meant it, but truth is I'd like to believe a lot of things that I now know are simply fiction.

After the photo was taken I remember Sofia explaining how disgusted she was of it and how the light didn't reflect off the lake like it should have. She handed the picture to me like she wanted me to hold on to it for the memories, but in reality she just wanted to have it removed from her sight.

I look at the photo now and all I feel is anger. I wish I would have seen everything that was coming. It's only after we lose the things we have, that we realize how ignorant we were to miss the signs that it was shortly leaving. I took a lighter out of my pocket and lit each of the four ends of the picture. I'd go back and forth from looking at the photo to looking at the lake and the spot where we were that day. The photo represents almost an entirely different era to me than present day. It has nothing to do with the climate change or the amount of leaves on the ground versus the amount of leaves on the tree. It has all to do with my mind set.

I consider myself crazy, but that's just me. I wouldn't care to listen to anyone else's opinion on my behavior or even a doctor's spiel on my diagnosis. I often wonder if I've always been crazy, crazy in the mind, doubtful, crazy in love, yes. Nevertheless I always had Sofia to counter the thoughts I expressed out loud. She would categorize my reaction using some concept she lived by to make all my actions sound acceptable and reasonable. Sofia was my own shrink, and that worked out perfectly for the both of us.

The sun was going down and the sky above me was changing into a variety of colors, something I may have had interest in before, but today it didn't mean shit. You may think that being with a photographer for over five years a man would gain some sort of respect for a sight like tonight however, towards the end, Sofia made it very clear that she wasn't as enthusiastic as she appeared to be.

Once the photo had burned into ashes I watched as it blew out of my hand and into the lake. I could see Sofia herself, burning the same photo. I felt like she had set up home inside my head, and was now laughing in my face.

A month ago I paid an unannounced visit to Sofia's apartment. Every time I've done this I've had a hidden agenda, a particular question I have wanted answered. On that day the question was "What do you see in all of these photos that you take?"

She let me in on the first ring, with a blank expression on her face; she must have known sooner or later I'd be at her door. I looked around her apartment; not much had changed. Photos were posted all over the walls and on top of the coffee table. Sofia was also into painting. She was very passionate about it, but she was never going to be good enough to make a career out of it, which is why she never tried to pursue it.

One of the paintings that caught my eye was a random canvas up against her leather couch with a variety of dark colors splashed across it. The painting really didn't remind me of something that

Sofia would paint, but again I was growing on the idea that Sofia wasn't much into her work.

"When did you paint that?"

Sofia put on a jacket to cover up her body as if I was some sort of old man trying to catch a nip slip.

Sofia while starring off into a corner replied, "Sometime ago, maybe last month" She brushed her hair with one hand. "Ollie why are you here?"

I sat down on her couch and looked at the developed pictures all across her coffee table, picking through them one by one.

"Because I want to know why." I had come over to her place a dozen times and asked the same foolish question.

Sofia sat down on a wooden chair opposite of me. "I'm just going to disregard that question."

I pulled out a cigarette and stuck it between my teeth.

Sofia blocked my hand when I reached for a lighter. "You can't smoke in here."

I put the cigarette on the coffee table. "Since when?"

Sofia picked up the cigarette and handed it back to me. "Since my apartment started smelling like an ashtray"

Sofia glanced down at the coffee table, she began turning over the photos she didn't want me to see. Before she could turn over one of them I picked it up and stared at it.

The photo was of a handsome man, maybe a model, maybe Sofia's new boyfriend.

"What do you see in all these photos you take?" I flipped the picture around so Sofia could see it.

"What do you mean?"

"I mean why did you take them? What about these people and things caught your eye?"

Sofia grabbed the photo out of my hand and glanced at it for only a few seconds before putting it back on the table.

"I don't know."

To be completely honest, I was getting quite irritated at Sofia avoiding my questions. She did it pretty often when we were together, but now that things had changed it seemed to fuck with me even more.

"How could you not know? You took them! You used your expensive little camera and you saw something; you must have seen something that made you want to take a picture."

Sofia began swiping the photos off of the coffee table and onto her Persian rug.

"You want to know what I see in them Ollie? You really want to know"?

"Yes, I really want to know."

"I see nothing in them; I simply push the button and take the fucking picture. I don't care for the sights in them or the people in them. They mean nothing to me. I just happen to be very good at it and I use that to my advantage."

Sofia stood up from her chair and looked at me.

"Maybe you should be taking advantage of what you have to offer and actually go somewhere in life."

"Maybe I like where I am."

"You mean everyone feeling sorry for you, constantly worried about how Ollie is doing today?"

"Sometimes I wonder how you're the same person I've been with all this time."

"*Were* with Ollie, the same person you *were* with?"

I stood up from the couch and headed toward the door. Somewhere between the couch and the door I realized this maybe the last time I ever enter her apartment again. I turned around and looked at her; she couldn't wait for me to leave her place.

"I wonder how I love you so much."

I called over a friend of mine that recently, I consider more of an acquaintance. In a small summary, he jumped the bandwagon that I had lost my mind. Sofia's and my friends weren't divided. They all decided to go with her, leaving me with no one on my side. I believe that's one of the many reasons I accepted defeat and isolation.

The friend was Mickey, Mickey Childs. The two of us sat on my stairs in front of my apartment smoking a bowl together. Mickey tossed over a handle of Vodka to me, and I proceeded to chug as much as I could within the first swig. My head felt like it was going to explode while my hands couldn't quit shaking.

I wasn't even in the mood for company. It was a last moment kind of thing and Mickey was in the neighborhood. Ironically, he had just left Sofia's apartment and was doing his best to avoiding answering any questions about how she was doing. I never had any interest in getting information from her friends about her. If anything, all I had to do was log on to Facebook and take a look at her profile. The technology world makes it much easier these days to feel depressed.

"I'm thinking about getting a place up in Norco."

"Why Norco?"

Mickey pushed back his long curly hair and stuck a cigarette between his lips.

"Rachael's been talking about getting a place together."

It was fascinating to be going through a hard time over a relationship and then have someone speak about how their life is perfectly set up. I obviously don't believe in something perfect, but I also understand that anything better than finding yourself detached to the rest of the population is as close to perfect as you can get.

"That didn't take very long. You sure you're ready with college on your chest?"

Mickey lights his cigarette.

"My parents are losing their business."

I was surprised that with the size of the town we were living in, and the quick spread of word of mouth, that I hadn't already heard this news. I did have to except the fact however that we weren't in high school anymore.

"I thought things were going well?"

"They are for right now, but let's be honest, who can afford the homes they have on the market right now. I knew shit was bad when my father asked me to come work with him."

Mickey passed me the lighter so I could light my cigarette.

"I don't want to start my life out on a sinking ship; I want to be a part of some big corporate company that I can put my name on someday."

I smoked my cigarette and waited as the conversation slowly died. Mickey and I continued to drink the Vodka and keep silence between us.

After about an hour, Mickey stood up and quickly grabbed the railing to keep himself from falling backwards. We were both three sheets to the wind. Mickey didn't hesitate to pull out his cell phone and call up a taxi.

Mickey shook my hand and started heading down the stairs, very carefully watching every one of his steps. When he reached the bottom he turned around and looked at me.

"You realize that it's socially impossible for you to communicate with anyone, right? Just because you're quiet doesn't mean everyone you used to hang out with can't tell you're falling apart. We tried . . ."

Mickey takes a puff of his cigarette.

"We tried so fucking hard to save you. I wish I would have kicked you in the ass a long time ago and told you to move on."

I put out my cigarette on the stair I was sitting on.

"No one ever understood what I had to say, whether I put it straight forward or explained it in stupid terms for people like you."

Mickey dropped his cigarette on the ground.

"I'll run into you sometime."

I took another hit of my cigarette.

"Yeah."

I turned the radio off in the car and picked up the envelope again. I opened it up. Inside was a photo of me. Sofia must have taken it when we first started going out. In the photo I was sitting on her bed wearing a hoodie. There was that expression again I thought I'd never see of me.

I flipped the photo around to see some writing I could quickly tell it was Sofia's. The letter read

"I see nothing in them;

I simply push the button and take the fucking picture.

I don't care for the sights in them or the people in them,

They mean nothing to me."

I set the picture down on the passenger seat. Within a few seconds the customer's came rushing out of the stores with the rain falling down hard on them. I turned my radio back on and put the car in reverse. I peeled out of the parking lot as quickly as the car allowed, as if everyone was reading the same letter.

In my rear view mirror Sofia stood glaring with the rest of the people I used to know.

# Chapter III

## The Apartment

After high school, I picked up an addiction to pain killers and muscle relaxants. I started taking oxycodone, hydrocodone, vicodin, and all the other thirty-one flavors. I was still living in the same apartment building and working at a mail processing warehouse. It became an easy convenience to come by all these drugs with my fellow coworkers. This didn't mean I had any sort of friendship with them; it just meant I had an infinite supply.

I'd spend my mornings before work drinking coffee and starring at the TV screen, watching some paid programming. I'd sit there for hours at a time. The only reason I'd get up is to vomit or grab some more pills. This episode wasn't coming from nowhere; I was headed in this direction for the past year.

There was very little furniture: a used couch, some old chairs, and a shitty refrigerator that was almost always empty. I was clearly broke. The only money I had would go towards rent and drugs, and believe me drugs would come first. I didn't mind having an argument with the landlord here and there.

I had made it a goal of mine to quit writing altogether. I no longer wanted to take a second look at my thoughts; once was plenty enough for me. You couldn't find a notebook or a script anywhere in my apartment. I had already burned all that shit in the trash and erased all my files off my computer. The only thing that remained on my hard drive was my music library. My taste of music these days was the likes of *"Modest Mouse"*, *"Neutral Milk Hotel"*, and *"Radiohead"*. Sometimes *"Dinosaur Jr."* would satisfy my ears as well.

Along with the music there was one other thing that remained on my laptop and that was a picture of Sofia. I kept one out of a thousand, and it wasn't even the best one of her, it was one of those feelings I came upon that I had to have one memory.

I entered the kitchen and poured myself a cup of coffee; I was on my second pot already. I lit up a cigarette at my writing desk and searched the internet for useless shit. Things I would never buy, places I would never go, and people I would never meet.

Inside my living room I turned the television on mute and put a record in, it was a revised album of *Neutral Milk Hotels' "In the Aeroplane Over the Sea"*. It was the album I normally had playing on my iPod when I used to write. I was just getting to the point where I could stomach listening to them without having a paper and pen in my hand or my fingers dancing around the keyboard on some screenplay program I had downloaded a few years ago.

I'd periodically glance at the TV and then go back to the computer, and then take a handful of oxy's. When my eyes started blurring, I'd go to the fridge and pull out a Corona. If it was after work, I'd grab a bottle off of the top of the refrigerator. Most nights it didn't matter what I was drinking; I'd still polish off the bottle. I'd drink anything from vodka to rum to some old whiskey. Booze, drugs, and cigarettes were all I spent my money on.

My car had started acting up about a month ago and I kept telling myself to bring it down to the shop that was no more than a couple of blocks from my house. I'd simply pass it on and make note to take care of it the next day. The other day I tried starting it, and the engine no longer turns.

There weren't too many distractions after I came home from work, I didn't talk to my neighbors and they didn't talk to me. A couple of times the cops would come by and tell me to turn down my music, but that was about it. They never suspected I was doing anything illegal, or maybe they could tell I was high as a kite but didn't give a shit because I was keeping to myself.

I realized how easily it was to destroy yourself when no one else was around or knew what you were up too. I kept a calm attitude at work, did my ten hours, and then came home. Luckily, I worked in the back of the store warehouse and didn't have to have any sort of communication with the customers. Right off the bat, my employer could tell I wasn't much one for communication and lacked social skills.

This life of seclusion was working for me. I was slowly deteriorating like I wanted and getting high when I wanted. There was no pressure of keeping people up to date with how I was doing or how I was feeling, like the shit that goes on Facebook. I was alone in my own solitary confinement, away from everything.

Then something happened. I woke up one day and decided I could rid myself of all the drugs and liquor in my system. I figured if I rounded up all the pills I had acquired over the past few months. I'd say goodbye to them and flush them down my toilet. I called off work on a Friday, and that's exactly what I did.

The pills where everywhere: in my cabinets, under my bed, in my desk drawers, in plastic containers, under the sink, and inside books on my shelf. Some were white, some were yellow, and some were blue. Some were uppers and some were downers. All of them were inside my apartment.

I had been starring at myself in the bathroom for several hours. In front of me, on top of the counter, was a mason jar full of assorted pills. I would every once in a while pick it up and look at it as if I were using a microscope. I wondered how something so little and so plain could give me such a high. Sure, there are a million scientific explanations as to why pills do what they do to the human body, but I wasn't interested in hearing any of them, nor would I ever try to have someone tell me how they work. All I simply knew is I'd put it on my tongue, grab a glass of whatever I was drinking, and swallow it. Within twenty to thirty minutes I would start feeling good. If not, I'd keep them coming till I did.

I never went to meetings. I never tried to get help, and no one ever convince me that I needed to stop. That was the beauty of being and living by myself without any other interactions. But, I felt inflicted. I felt an unusual guilt that this wasn't right. This isn't how someone should live their life, especially not a twenty year old who's just fresh out of high school.

The only way I justified my habits and my addiction was by lying to myself that this wasn't all about a girl. This wasn't Sofia winning and me becoming a pill popper. She lived her life in a different style with different coping skills that were actually healthy. Then again, what did she need coping skills for? Her childhood wasn't that bad. Her parents were still together and paying for her college intuition. Forgive me, she worked part time at a grill off of Del Rio once or twice a week so she and her friends could walk over to the mall and shop for ridiculous items.

I also lied to myself when I said I didn't think or care about her anymore. If I didn't care about her anymore, than I wouldn't still have a fucking picture of her with me at all times. Constantly taking it out, like some Vietnam vet looking at a picture of a soldier who died beside him in the war.

"Fuck it" I said and flushed all of the pills down the toilet.

In my living room I kept a map of the United States on my wall. The entire New England area was circled in dark red. It was a place I dreamed of living someday, way out there in the woods. I'd build myself a cabin and have a shed full of liquor at my expense. Most importantly I would have silence.

I often dreamed of what I would do with all that area to myself and no one else to share it with. I planned on cutting wood for the fire in the morning, rolling my tobacco periodically through the day, hunting for deer with my rifle, and fishing with a pole. At night I'd sit by a fire that I started. I would live in a cabin that I had built with my own two hands.

Most people couldn't live in conditions like that. They would fall into cabin fever too quickly. These people are considered the majority. Some people, however, consider silence their first language and isolation their natural habitat; these people are the minority. And the way I see it is, I have always been one for isolation and pure silence. These days conversation, to me, seems useless; it goes on forever and is headed nowhere. I'd rather be without it.

Around 5 p.m., I started feeling the withdrawals coming along. I looked around the apartment for something sweet, but I couldn't come up with anything more than a bag full of old Swedish fish. I had a couple of them and threw the rest away in the trash.

Two months ago I had a visit from Sofia. She came over unannounced just like I had done to her several times. However, my reaction was a little different than hers. I unlocked the door for her and immediately went back to the couch as if I didn't even recognize her.

"I see you're living quite well"

I continued to not talk and switched the channel on the TV to some sports show recapping a football game.

"I heard you were working at Pitney's."

"What about it?"

Sofia walked closer to the couch and picked up an empty bottle of tequila, in an observant kind of way.

"You sure you aren't just trying to get back at me?"

"Get back at you for what?"

Sofia set the empty bottle down; I sat up straight on the couch.

"Don't try an act like you didn't know Emma works there."

I stuck a cigarette between my lips.

"What does that have to do with anything?"

I lit the cigarette.

"You can't be with me, so now you're going for one of my friends."

Sofia was out of her mind. I knew Emma worked there, but I didn't pay much attention to her and there especially wasn't any attraction between us.

"Yeah that's exactly it. Did you figure that out all on your own?"

"I want you to stay away from me and I want you to stay away from my friends."

I noticed there was some rum left in a glass from last night; I helped myself to a drink.

"Sure. I'll just give them my notice."

Sofia could easily sense the sarcasm in my voice and it didn't help the situation any.

"Why can't you get a life of your own? Why can't you just go somewhere fucking else?"

Purposely ignoring Sofia's statement, I looked down at the table and realized I was out of liquor.

"Shit. I'm all out."

I stood up from the couch and began heading for the kitchen to get more booze when Sofia stepped in front of me.

"I'm sorry I couldn't keep faking my feelings for you. Sooner or later I had to quit worrying about you and start doing what makes me happy."

I walked around Sofia and into the kitchen; on the refrigerator, I still had plenty of bottles for the rest of the night. I was doing my best to keep my composure. I pulled out a dirty glass from the sink and poured some Johnny Walker in it.

I drank the few inches of whiskey within a second. I reached back to the bottle and poured myself another glass. This time, I poured more than just a few inches. I quickly drank the whiskey. I was starting to feel the effects of the liquor; at the time, it was the only thing keeping me stable. I grabbed the bottle again, but this time, instead of pouring it into a glass; I chose to drink it from the bottle. I heard the front door shut; Sofia had finally decided to leave.

Through the night I continued to drink away. I had taken the initiative earlier to stop taking pills I never made any sort of agreement about quitting alcohol. I felt as long as I kept drinking, everything would be fine. In this sort of situation, with events similar to todays, I would have already been on my fourth line, snorting some oxy's or some vike's. Despite all of the madness, I actually believed I was making progress with myself.

Within the next couple of hours, I started the destruction phase, as I would like to call it. I began tearing up my apartment, going from room to room ripping things off the wall, pulling bookshelves

22

apart, breaking my table. At one point, I reached in the sink to grab a glass so I could throw it. I was so angry that I broke the glass in my hand and watched as the blood dripped down from the little pieces digging into my skin.

I didn't attempt to take care of it or wrap it in anything. Around this time I was starting to stumble, heading for a black out.

I walked over to my entertainment center and pulled out a DVD labeled "Holland 1945" a reference to the song of the same name by *Neutral Milk Hotel*. I very clumsily put the DVD in and turned on the TV. I somehow managed to make my way back on to the couch. That's when I remembered something; I had stashed underneath the couch a bag of oxy's. I fell on to the floor and reached under the couch barely grabbing ahold of the bag with my fingertips.

I tore the bag open, spilling pills everywhere and started taking handfuls at a time. I didn't even realize I was relapsing. To me, this was a normal end of my nightly routine. I was simply following the same pattern as usual; except, on this night, I had taken way more than ever before.

As I sat on the couch drunk, high, and bleeding severely from the cuts on my hand, I watched the old DVD of Sofia and me. We had taken turns shooting film of each other one Christmas Eve. She was beautiful, as always, wearing an elegant red dress. I was wearing some Indie band shirt that was a present from her.

The DVD went on for about forty five minutes; it was as if I could remember everything that happened that night from start to finish. It was our third Christmas spent together and it still felt like our first. I began thinking about what Sofia had mentioned earlier about "faking her feelings". I wondered if that was what she was doing since the beginning, and that Christmas, or if that was just something she made up to make me feel like shit.

The more I saw myself smiling in the video, the angrier I grew. The more I saw her smiling in the video, the sicker I grew. I realized something else as I was watching it. Not once in the whole forty five minutes of the video were Sofia and I together. There were dozens of people at that party; any one of them could have taken over the camera.

I began feeling even weaker and soon enough the video was only a blur. I had lost feeling in my hand; as a matter of fact, I had lost feeling of my entire body. I was finished. I was through. I was dying.

# Chapter IV

## Old English

I woke up and was out of bed around 7 a.m. It was beginning to get sunny, so I opened up the blinds. I walked down stairs into the kitchen and put on a new pot of coffee. I lit myself a cigarette and watched the birds all fly towards the trees.

I walked out of my house in my robe, with my cigarette hanging from the side of my mouth. The house I was now living in was a two story home built in the early sixties. It had its problems, but it gave me something to do in my spare time, when I wasn't working at the hardware store.

The driveway was long, stretching out at least twenty feet from the garage. I walked down it in my house slippers to pick up the day's paper. The title of the cover story read <u>"October is here"</u>.

The date was Oct 21'st 2014, and it was Monday. I took a quick look around the neighborhood to see if anything had changed. Dead leaves covered almost all the houses' front lawns. I turned around and walked back inside.

I set the paper down on the table and began to cook up some eggs and bacon for the morning's breakfast.

In the upstairs bedroom, in a different room than mine, laid Sofia Mertzon still asleep in her bed. The two of us had gotten back together, engaged, and married all in the same weekend. It was our second year together as husband and wife.

Very early on in our marriage we decided it would be best for the both of us if we each had our own room with our own bed. Things seemed to be working between us with this kind of set up.

Sofia woke up around 8:30 a.m. and headed downstairs to find me reading the paper at the kitchen table on my third cup of coffee. I looked up at her and smiled.

"Good morning."

She walked over and hugged me from behind and then kissed me on the top of my head.

"Good morning."

She smelt the food I cooked and walked over to the stove.

"What did you make for breakfast?"

"Some eggs and bacon. You want some?"

Sofia opened up the fridge.

"No, I'm fine. I'll just have a bagel."

Sofia sat down at the table right next to me and waited until I looked up.

"How is your leg doing?"

"It's a lot better."

Sofia was referring to an injury I had suffered while in the navy. After my overdose and months of rehab, I had decided to join the Navy and become a sailor. This decision may seem completely left field; however, the military ran all through my family. My father was in the navy, his father was in the navy, and even my great uncle was in both the navy and the coast guard.

Unfortunately, I became the first one to be injured. During a standard Man Over drill aboard a navy vessel, I had lost my balance while standing on the railing of the ship. Somewhere along the line,

I managed to get my foot stuck in a rope. Once the first wave came crushing into the ship, I fell off and immediately was hung upside down by my left leg.

The injury was severe enough to make me unfit for duty. I was honorably discharged within a couple of months. With the money I received from the Navy, I decided to buy myself my own place up in the New England area, like I had always wanted.

To be quite honest, how Sofia and I winded up back together all happened pretty fast. She had heard of my injury from one of my fellow shipmates who contacted my folks. Without much discussion, she told me that she wanted to come take care of me. Even though I hated the thought of being taken care of, I agreed. Within a week the two of us were living together and within a month the two of us were married.

Before marriage we made some stipulations that we thought were for the better, one of which was having separate beds.

The marriage felt stable. It was the first time since our high school years that we were able to function together without having any arguments and disputes. We kept the details of our marriage very secretive. We knew if we involved anyone else in it, the marriage wouldn't work out. This included counselors.

Sofia lifted up the table cloth to see my leg.

"You mind if I take a look at it?"

I lifted up my leg as high as I could to show her. The only time I really felt pain was when it was higher than my other leg. Sofia didn't know much in the medical field, but she tried her best to read books and become more educated on certain subjects.

"It's not as swollen as normal."

Sofia rubbed her hand across my leg, massaging it.

"Does it hurt right now?"

I sighed, "Only a little bit."

Sofia leaned down and kissed my leg.

"Is that any better?"

I smiled at her and put my leg back on the ground.

"Much better."

Another stipulation between Sofia and I, was that we would each have our alone time. I would spend mine in the garage either working out or watching the football game. I had become a Patriots fan overnight.

I would put on the stereo system and listen to music. These days I was in the taste of *Iron and Wine*, *Jack Johnson*, and *Band of Horses*, Bands that would allow me to relax when I needed too, and keep me in the right mind set.

I kept a fridge in the garage filled only with water and juice. Alcohol was no longer in my house. There were plenty of days when I thought about having a drink or going down to the local bar, but the urge would pass. Sofia also was going without drinking. It was an effort, she said, and we both had to take part in it for it to work.

When the alcohol ads would come on the TV during the game I would have to change the channel. I tried once to sit through a commercial and it almost pushed me to picking up the bottle again. I figured someday I'd be able to watch and it would have no effect on me, but I wasn't there just yet.

Sofia would normally sew something or be reading while I was either away at work or going to the store. I never asked her why she started sewing just like she never asked me why I would go to the garage.

At the end of the day we'd sit at the table and have dinner. Our conversations were mostly over the news or some gossip she had heard from the neighbors. We would finish the night off with some dessert and discuss our plans for the following day, whether she needed the car or if she could have one of the neighbors take her to the local market.

We'd kiss each other and she'd normally go to bed first. Sometimes I'd think about going into her room and lying next to her. It was strange not watching her fall asleep or waking up beside her. Like all things, it took some getting used to. If the temptation was too much then I'd go for a walk. I'd just keep walking till something else came to my mind, and then I'd go back home. Some nights I was out until the sun started coming up.

Working at the hardware store wasn't too much of a burden. Every once in a while I would carry on a conversation with one of the townspeople, but most of them knew I kept to myself and was mainly quiet. I'm sure they probably just thought I had always been that way and was a mild mannered man. No one ever asked questions about Sofia's and my marriage and if they did, I would quickly change the topic.

One afternoon while smoking my cigarette, I noticed a health magazine on the table. It must have been Sofia's. For some odd reason I picked it up and began reading through it. Since, I had pretty much gotten all the information I needed from the days paper.

As I was flipping through the Magazine I began seeing ad after ad for pain medication. Immediately my mind was controlled by familiar names like oxycodone, and vicodin, and Valium. It seemed like every page in the magazine had some sort of medication listed. When I reached the end of the magazine I tore it up and threw it in the trashcan.

My mind started going back and forth from when I was addicted and to the present. I started having bizarre thoughts. It was almost like I saw myself as a joke as if I picked up some sort of persona that was completely fake. This person I was pretending to be was all a gimmick.

If I had a mirror in front of me, I would see someone else. I was trapped in a body with a mind that wasn't mine. What was I doing? Why was I living with a wife that I didn't sleep with? Why did I have a fridge full of water and not ice cold beer? Why was it the only sort of pill you would find in my house was a fucking vitamin? Why wasn't I drunk right now? Why wasn't I high right now?

I went into the living room to find Sofia sitting on the couch sewing a pair of jeans.

"Hey honey."

I just continued to stand there and stare at her.

"Are you okay? Is your leg bothering you?

I surprised myself when I started to cry. I felt a tear roll down my cheeks.

"Ollie you're scaring me."

I took a step backwards.

"Who are we?"

Sofia put down the pair of jeans and needle.

"What do you mean?"

"I mean, who are we? What is this?"

"What is what?"

Sofia stood up and began walking towards me. I took another step back as if I didn't recognize who she was, like she was a stranger living inside my house.

"Is there something you want to talk about?"

I turned around and headed for the garage.

I sat in my chair with the TV off and my music on; Sofia hadn't followed me into the garage. I don't know whether it was because she was scared or because she thought I needed time alone. I was just happy she didn't.

Suddenly all the events that happened so fast and landed me here started rushing through my mind. My time in the service felt like it went by so fast, it seemed to me as if I had never really processed everything. I just woke up one day and believed that this life was fine, that it was normal.

It wasn't the rehab or the therapists, or the shitty groups that I went too that stopped me from drinking and popping pills. It was the time I had spent on the ship with people who knew nothing about my past. It was the time I had spent away from Sofia.

I don't remember what happened after that night I overdosed. I only remember what she had told me. How could she know all the details, she wasn't even there? What if she was just feeding me lies off of a silver platter and I was happily biting into them? There was no possible way I could know the truth. I had no way of knowing what happened except for trusting the words from the mouth of a women who had wanted me to go somewhere fucking else. And that's exactly what I did. This whole entire time I've been listening to her, letting her control my every move.

I missed the ship; I missed being surrounded by nothing but water. Now that I was on land, my choices had become no longer my choices. I knew I wasn't losing it; at this moment I had the clearest vision and I was the only one inside my mind.

I opened up the fridge once more hoping there would be a fresh beer, even just one. Maybe I had stashed one somewhere in a box or plastic bin like I had stashed the pills under the couch that night.

I came back inside the house and headed for the kitchen. The first place I looked was on top of the refrigerator, but only a pile of plastic plates and paper cups were there. I began opening up all the drawers and cabinets, only to find silverware, pots, and pans. Somewhere, I had to have stashed something; I always did.

Sofia came into the kitchen and saw me desperately looking for something.

"Ollie please tell me what is going on?"

"Where did I put it?"

I kept repeating over and over to myself these words. I wasn't going to give up until I had my hands on a bottle. I didn't care if it was cheap vodka or boxed wine.

"What are you looking for?"

I was getting to the point of frustration and began pulling the drawers all the way out and on to the floor.

"Stop it!"

Right when Sofia spoke I quit moving. It was obvious she had stashed it and she knew where it was.

"Where did you put it?"

"Where did I put what?"

I punched a cabinet to my right, making Sofia jump back in fear.

"The alcohol! The drugs! Where did you put them all?"

"We've been over this. There isn't any in the house, remember?"

I walked closer to Sofia until she wasn't any more than a few inches in front of me.

"I'm going to make sure you can perfectly hear me . . . where did you put them all?"

Sofia put her hand over her mouth in fear. She saw me as some kind of monster and I knew it. I had seen that look on her face before and many others just like it.

"I don't know"

I slapped Sofia in the face as hard as I could. She didn't say a word; she just kept her hand over her face for protection.

"Is that all it took this whole time to make you silent, for me to hit you?"

Sofia still didn't say anything.

"After all the times of me falling to my knees and begging you to stay? Or how about all the times you came over just to tell me how much you hated me?"

I slapped her again on the other side of her face. Her eyes became watery, but still as I had predicated, she was silent.

"I finally see how good it feels to hurt someone you don't love anymore."

I left the house and headed for the bar down the street that I had passed so many times before while coming home from work. When I walked in, it smelt of booze and cigarettes. Our town had one of the very few bars left that allowed smoking.

I took a spot at the bar and waited for the bartender to approach me; it wasn't too busy, so it didn't take very long. I ordered myself a glass of whiskey with no ice. The bartender could tell I was in a hurry to get drunk, and quickly brought me my drink.

I lit myself a cigarette and paid no attention to anyone else; people came and went all night long. I found myself starring at a mirror in front of me where the liquor was kept. The mirror was large enough that I could see my face. I looked like I was fifty years old and felt like a hundred.

I thought back to what Sofia said while we were in the kitchen. What had she meant when she said "We've been over this." I wondered if this wasn't the first time I've acted like this. And if so did it ever go this far? How many times while living in that house had I discovered I was somebody else and that everything was a lie. Had she ever once came out and told the truth to me? And if she did, why didn't I remember? Why do I keep making the same mistake over the same woman?

As the night passed on, I continued drinking whiskey. The bartender could see that I was trashed, but I wasn't causing any problems so he continued to pour. I smoked through two packs of cigarettes while sitting at the bar.

When the time came to close the bar down, I paid my tab and walked out. The bartender offered a ride home, but I told him I'd prefer to walk. I wasn't lying. I walked right past my truck and headed for home.


I woke up in the morning of October 22nd on my couch. Despite the amount of alcohol has I had consumed the night before, I still remembered everything that had happened. I expected that Sofia had left to go stay at a friend's house and wanted nothing to do with me.

I walked into the kitchen to make a cup of coffee and was shocked to see the kitchen was all cleaned up. There was no broken glass or pulled out cabinets; everything was put back in its right place. Not only that, but a fresh pot of coffee was being made.

I walked upstairs and into Sofia's bedroom to find her standing in front of a mirror holding a dress in front of her. She turned around and smiled at me.

"Do you think this would look good on me?

I was flabbergasted. First off, I didn't think she'd still be in the same house as me and second off, she was smiling. I could still see the marks on her face from where I had hit her, but she had done her best to cover it up with make-up.

"I've got a job interview this morning and I still don't know what to wear."

Sofia picked up another dress off of the bed and put it in front of her.

"Or do you think this one looks more appropriate? After all, I'm going to be working around children."

I shook my head at her.

"I think they both look nice."

Sofia turned back around in front of the mirror and began posing with the dress. I was in a land of confusion and decided to head back down stairs.

After about half an hour Sofia came walking down stairs in the red dress she had picked out. She picked up her purse and walked over to me.

"I put some fresh coffee on for you. I'm sorry I didn't have time to make anything to eat, but the school just called me for this interview.

Sofia leaned down and kissed me on the lips.

"I love you."

She stood back up and walked out the door, leaving me with my head spinning with thoughts.

# Chapter V

## The Light I can never turn off

It's late at night and nothing is opened. The street lights are all off. There are cars all on the road but nobody is in them. I'm walking around looking for a house that I've once been to; however, I can't remember where that house is.

The cold starts to hit my skin and I can't keep warm. Suddenly I start losing my memory to time: all the memories of the good weekends, the best friends, and the people I love. All the clouds are clouding my judgment and the choices I make. I'm not just looking for an exit but I'm looking for a new path.

I start to get a headache, the worst headache I've ever had. My eyes are getting worse every second, when finally I see a home that looks familiar. There is a light coming from this house, so I walk to it and open the door. The house is quiet. I can tell no one else is inside it but me. For some reason, I decided to head up stairs and go into the bedroom. Standing around in the bedroom I realize that this is my own bedroom. I figure out that the light is coming from behind a door. I go to open the door, but it's locked. I've finally found the light I was looking for, but it's the light in the closet I can never turn off.

# Chapter VI

## Little Motel

Sofia unbuttoned her shirt in front of a man who promised to pay her twenty dollars. The man was twice her age and had picked her up on the side of the street outside of a Denny's. He had rolled down his window and she asked him if he wanted a good time. The man had become accustom to this sort of deal before.

Sofia was aware that the man would want to see more, so she button back up her shirt and told him to drive to the nearest motel. He did as she asked. The man found the cheapest motel possible a couple miles down from the Denny's. The sign of the motel could barely be seen. It took a second look to read, "Wayside Inn."

It was raining hard outside, so the man told Sofia to wait in the car as he went to the front office and bought a room for the night.

Once the room was paid for, she stepped outside the car and hurried over to where the man was standing at room #10.

The motel room smelt of cigarettes and booze. The carpet was partially coming up, there was no fridge, the TV didn't work, and the bed sheets had stains of only god knows what all over them.

"What now?" The anxious man said.

Sofia knew what she had to do if she wanted him to pay well. She would have to be his little play doll.

"I'm here for you baby. We can do whatever you want."

Sofia could barely stomach the words that were coming out of her own mouth. The man smiled. He had maybe half a full set of teeth.

"Well alright then."

The man put his hands on Sofia's breast and squeezed them both hard. She tried looking up at the ceiling to distract herself from what was going on, but the man moved his hand to her chin and pulled her in for a kiss. He also smelt terribly of cigarettes and booze.

"You're a dirty girl aren't you?"

Sofia could only imagine what this man was planning to do to her.

She repeated herself from before.

"I'm whatever you want me to be."

The man reached down and unzipped his pants. Sofia knew sooner or later she would have to act like she was interested in him. She took off her shirt once more; she had no bra on underneath.

The man wrapped both his hands around her neck and forced her head towards his exposed crotch. He shoved himself inside her and began to groan.

This was what Sofia's life had become. She was no longer blessed with a life of riches; she no longer had a place to call her home.

After the man had gotten everything he wanted out of her, he opened up his wallet and stuck fifty dollars down her shirt.

"You can stay here for the rest of the night."

She pretended to smile as well as she could. He opened up the door and walked out.

This wasn't the first time Sofia had had sex for money. In the past month alone, she had done a number of sexual acts for anywhere between twenty to a hundred dollars. By now, she was used to getting paid nothing.

Sofia stepped inside the bathroom and turned on the shower. She had forgotten how long it had been since she had a warm shower. Her clothes were dirty and hadn't been washed in weeks. After her long shower she headed down to the laundry room and used some of the money she had earned that night to clean her clothes.

Sofia crossed the street and bought a pack of cigarettes and a sandwich from the gas station. She walked back to the motel parking lot and lit up the cigarette. It was five in the morning; the sun would be coming up any minute now.

She couldn't help but wonder what she had done to end up where she was at. Not in a million years could she ever see herself doing the things she was doing now.

Sofia often thought about me. She had no idea where I had gone to, what I was doing, or if I was even still alive. She had come to the realization that life with me wasn't as awful as she thought, and that there were many things that could be worse.

After her cigarette, she got her clothes out of the laundry and went to bed. She had six hours before she had to check out and find somewhere else to sleep for the next night. While she lay in bed that morning, she thought about what would happen if we got back together, if she could ever come to grips with telling me the horrible things she had done for money, and if I would even consider the idea of taking her back.

She woke up to a knock at the door. She quickly put on her clothes and looked through the peephole; it was the cleaning lady.

She gathered up all her things and left. She knew that eventually she would have to pick a different venue than Denny's. By now, some of the employees had to catch on that she was a prostitute. On occasions, the manager would come out and ask her what she was doing. Her answer was always the same "I'm waiting for a ride," which sadly, wasn't a lie.

Sofia looked inside her purse. She had forty one dollars left and some change. She knew it wasn't enough to get her another room at even the shitty motel she stayed at the night before. What could she possibly do with forty one dollars?

Sofia thought back to a time when she was still getting money from her father. That was before he had remarried and taken on three extra kids. Once he had done that, he stopped giving her allowance for her shopping sprees and before she knew it, he had stopped paying her college tuition. She was only a few courses away from graduating with a bachelor's degree in business management, but with no prior job other than working at the Grill for one summer, no one in their right mind would give her a loan or a grant. Plus, even if she was to somehow pull of getting a loan, where would she stay? There was no way she could afford to live in the dorms.

Sofia thought about maybe living with one of her college friends, but she was to stubborn to reach out and tell them she was flat out broke. And what if they rejected her? She didn't want the whole campus knowing she was going around asking people for a place to stay.

Thinking of all this reminded her of back in high school when I was having a conversation with her about the importance of college. She was stressing to me how having a college degree was everything in the real world. I was asking what her definition was of the real world. She thought long and hard for a couple of minutes but was unable to spit out even one word.

I was always challenging her with questions like that and she did her best to answer them, but never could. Eventually she would avoid them all together and begin talking about something else.

I wasn't trying to tell her that college was a complete waste of time and money, but it's not everything. There are by far more worthy traits then having a college degree and that goes for any field. She couldn't comprehend my point of view though, so I let her have the last word, as always.

There had always existed a fine line between Sofia and I and not even the two of us could figure out where it was located. My best guess was that I saw the art in something and she only saw the value. It didn't matter if she had a good eye in photography or not. She'd never pursue it more than a hobby.

I also suffered from the same effect. I would never take my writing to newer heights because it didn't matter what I wrote. It always revolved around Sofia. I related my characters to her. She was at the center of all my stories. It happened so often that I didn't even realize when I was doing it. It had got to the point where I just couldn't function anymore. After we broke up, it hurt to even pick up a paper and pen. I was sick of looking at a reflection. It was causing more damage in my life than good. And like Sofia, I had to let it go.

Sofia was down to ten dollars. She made a stop by the payphone. She was surprised there were still payphones around. She made a phone call to my cell phone. By this time I was headed out North to the mountains where there wasn't a signal for miles. She left a message, "I could never leave you." She hung up shortly after. She stood at the payphone for quite some time before deciding to make one final phone call; it was to her mother still living in California.

When she heard her mother's voice on the other line it hit her like a ton of bricks. She started to cry. It took her mother a couple seconds to recognize it was her daughter since she hadn't spoken to her in so long. Sofia explained what had happened, but still left certain details out that she wished her mother would never find out about. She would take those secrets to the grave with her.

Sofia's mother flew out that night to see her. The two of them had breakfast and caught up on the past. They took a flight together back to California. Sofia didn't have the slightest idea of what was next.

After a couple weeks her mother broke the news that I was still living in New England. Sofia's mother encouraged her daughter to try and refocus on what she wanted most in life and see if it was in her to love again.

# Chapter VII

## The Winter Cabin

After giving it a good thought for quite some time, I decided I needed to get away. For the past few months, I had been struggling with who I really was as a husband and as a human being. I headed for the mountains up north where it was still snowing. When Sofia asked why I had to leave, I couldn't give her an answer. After reacting the way that she did to me hitting her, there was no way she could comprehend why I had to escape.

I had imagined living up in the mountains in a small cabin ever since I was in high school and now I needed to be there more than ever. I desperately needed the time alone to come up with a conclusion about who I was inside and out.

Having lived in the cabin for two weeks now, I realized that there is more than just one layer to a man. There were several layers that I had yet to discover about myself. The only thing I knew for certain was that I had to discover them by myself and without anyone's help. That way I wouldn't be confused as to what those layers contained. Most importantly, I had to leave in order for Sofia to be safe. Who knows what I am capable after that night? If I was going to destroy myself out here in mountains, then at least I would only be destroying myself and no one else.

I didn't know if part of the reason I left was because I loved her or not. Typically you don't try and destroy the things you love. I wasn't sure if I loved anything anymore or if I had ever loved anything at all. That might be a common excuse for someone to use who has trust issues, but for me it *was* the truth.

I spent the morning of December 11, 2014, cutting up firewood for the week. The winter temperatures were below freezing and I had waited until the last second to prepare. I was out there for a good four hours chopping away. I'd take a break here and there to have a cigarette. I would have to light the cigarette two to three times every smoke just to keep it lit.

I went inside the cabin and started up a fire. I was able to keep the cabin warm by placing comforters and wool all around. The cabin wasn't any bigger than a few hundred square feet, but it was all I needed.

The winter was hitting harder than I had expected and I was very quickly running out of food. I reached inside the cabinet above the stove and found only a few more cans of soup left. I never gave myself a date of when I was returning home, therefore, I didn't bring enough of what I should.

I sat on the floor next to the fire place and ate the soup of chicken noodles right out of the can. Afterwards, I threw the can in the fireplace and lit myself another cigarette.

I walked into the kitchen and pulled a bottle of Johnny Walker off the refrigerator. Booze was about the only thing I still had in great supply. I proceeded to get drunk that night, just like the ones before it. In my mind, I was going over scenarios on how to survive. I knew that I would most likely not make it another week in the conditions I was living without food. Also, the river was completely frozen.

I continued to drink from the bottle thinking it would give me some kind of idea on how to get myself out of the situation in which I was stuck. After brainstorming, I realized there was only one solution.

I opened up the closet near the front door and pulled out my Winchester. I had only gone shooting a few times in the Navy and to my memory, I didn't do so well.

At the bottom of the closet was a box full of ammunition for the rifle. I bought the ammo and the rifle awhile back when I was in the Navy. I had brought it up to the cabin for protection. I wasn't expecting to use it. It had been awhile since I qualified with a weapon and that wasn't anywhere close to a Winchester.

I packed up a few things in my old ruck sack including some extra socks, gloves, shirts, etc. I didn't have any food to bring, only a bottle of Old Crow.

I put the rucksack next to the front door and set my rifle right beside it, the ammo was already tucked away. I decided I would leave in the early morning and sleep off my drink.

Morning came sooner than I thought it would. I did my daily routine and poured myself a cup of black coffee and smoked my first cigarette. I made sure I rolled enough to last me a couple of days. I had no idea how long I would be out there and quite honestly I had no idea if I would make it back.

I was hunting for a deer. I tried remembering the last time I had seen one come this way. It might have been a week ago when I was sitting on my porch; I had no intention of killing it then. To me, it seemed like just another creature roaming the land for a place to lay its head.

This morning felt colder than the rest. I hadn't ever spent more than a few hours outside the cabin in fear of catching a cold or worse hypothermia. The boots I was wearing weren't even meant for the cold conditions that I was under. I'm not sure any of the clothing I was wearing was appropriate for what I was encountering.

I wasn't quite sure what this hunt meant to me, but it had to be more than just a quest for food. Where was my mind when I decided to come out here, or was that the entire purpose of my journey: to see what I was made of, to see what I would do with no support and no contact with anyone else, to be completely cut off from the rest of the civilization.

I looked up at the sun and tried to think of how much time I had left until it was night. I was a fool for never paying attention to it while I was back at the cabin.

I took a break and leaned up against a tree high in the mountains. I had traveled about four miles already. I grabbed my leg; I was starting to feel pain in it again. With everything that was going on around me, I somehow manage to forget I had a weak leg. How could I be so sidetracked as to not remember?

I heard a series of cracks not too far from where I was standing. I quickly turned around and tried to see what made them. I picked up my rifle hoping it was something I could kill. I took my ruck sack off and set it on the ground. I began pacing towards the noise, trying to be as stealthy as I could. Out of the corner of my eye, I saw an object moving fast. I held up my rifle and moved towards it. Once my eyes connected with the object, I could tell it was only a bird, but before I knew it I stepped into a steep hole and fell sideways, hitting my head on a stump and knocking me unconscious.

Through the next couple of minutes, my eyes would open and then shut. I tried to get my leg loose, but it wouldn't give. I was tired and defeated; I simply closed my eyes and waited for death.

While unconscious, I thought back to when I was on the Navy vessel. More distinctly, when I was looking over the soldiers we were transporting back to the states. Most of them were in critical condition and wouldn't make it even to shore. This wasn't my regular duty; I was simply filling in for another shipmate.

I remember one soldier in particular and the conversation I had with him while he lay on a hospital bed slowly dying. His name was Lieutenant Schroeder. He had been shot several times and was on his way to losing both his legs.

I stood in the corner of the ship and did my best not to stare at any of them. I believed they wanted as much space and as much fresh air as they could get before they passed.

Lieutenant Schroeder looked over at me. I was only a Private then. This was before my accident and I hadn't been in the service any longer than a couple of months.

"What's your name?"

I looked over at him with his body seeming almost lifeless.

"Pvt. Magnum, Sir."

"Why do you look like you've never seen someone die before?"

I kept silent, unable to answer his question. The last thing I wanted to do was offended him.

"Let me guess, it is your first time, isn't it?

I nodded my head.

"Yes Sir."

He laughed in a sad manner.

"It's a shame you're fighting this war."

"No disrespect, Sir, but I've been properly trained."

The Lieutenant shook his head.

"I'm not questioning your level of training son; I'm speaking of your age."

"I'm twenty-three, Sir."

The Lieutenant laughed again and probably thought back to when he was twenty-three.

"You're only twenty-three; I'm fifty-four years old. I've seen what this world has to offer. This is probably your first time out of your home state. Am I right?

I nodded my head in agreement.

"You have a woman back home?"

"She's not my woman anymore, Sir."

"Do you love her?"

This was the first time in a while since I had come aboard the vessel that I actually thought of Sofia.

"I imagine I love her too much."

The Lieutenant looked me straight in the eyes like I was last person he'd ever see.

"You can never love anything too much, son. Everyone fights a war within themselves, a war deep inside their heart. One that when you talk about it, it makes your hands shake while you hold up a glass. Never succumb to that war. As long as you fight it, you can never truly die."

I listened to every word the Lieutenant was telling me and remained standing still as he slowly closed his eyes and passed on, playing his words over and over again my head.

I woke up falling to the ground with my leg swinging out of the hole. There was blood in the snow from where I hit my head on the stump. It was morning again; I had spent the entire night out here in the cold.

My leg was in agonizing pain and I was pretty positive it was broken. Thankfully, I still had my Winchester beside me within my arm's reach. My ruck sack was lying on the ground, almost buried in the snow. I most likely suffered a concussion from the fall because my head was pounding like the beat of a drum. On top of everything, I was coughing which gave me reason to believe I had caught a cold.

I was able to pick up my rifle, but I wasn't even sure if I could use it. How much strength did I have left? I was four miles away from the cabin, still with no food. If I didn't come up of with a plan fast, I was certain I wouldn't make it another night.

I began crawling with my rifle in front of me tucked between my arms. There was no reason to keep carrying around my rucksack; it would only slow me down and make it that much harder to crawl through the snow. The only guidance I had was my own foot tracks. I decided I would try going back the way I came on only my hands and feet. I estimated I would get no further than a mile.

An hour had passed and there was no telling how far I had traveled. I knew it was still a long distance. I was too afraid to turn around in fear of seeing my rucksack and realizing I was getting nowhere.

Why had I thought about Lieutenant Schroeder? My memory of him was considerably unpleasant and I had suppressed it ever since I stepped off that vessel. I never shared the conversation I had with him to anybody else, not even his family. You would think a man's last words would sound completely different. I was waiting for him to give me a letter addressed to his wife or to his son, not words of wisdom to a young Private he had never known. I felt selfish about the whole thing. His words didn't mean anything to me and Lieutenant Schroeder had wasted his final minutes talking to practically a wall.

There was no one around to hear my last words. There was no letter in my pocket. This was my punishment and it didn't matter if I was ready to except it or not; the end was unavoidable.

I heard another series of cracks almost in the same order as earlier. I looked up and saw a deer a couple of meters in front of me. I held out my rifle and went into the prone position. Through the scope I could clearly see the deer bright as day, standing still. I inhaled, exhaled, and then fired. The deer fell down simultaneously. I watched through the scope as the deer struggled to stand back up. After a few seconds, the deer stopped fighting. I assumed it was dead. I stopped from crawling any further and laid down my rifle. The winter could have me.

A seasoned hunter followed my tracks through the snow. The town had put a temporally ban on hunting I was never informed of or sought out. I had failed to even register with the wildlife office. If I had, then I wouldn't be stuck in this position. Someone down in the office, or maybe even someone living in the mountains not too far from here, must have heard the shot.

I wasn't sure how I felt about someone finding me. Maybe my whole purpose was to die out here. It seemed like I had spent that last few years going into corners with no possible exit, but once again I found a way out.

# Chapter VIII

## The Bedroom

I woke up next to Sofia lying in my bed. I was back at our home in New England. It was hard to believe we were in the same bed together again. Sofia was kissing my cheek and breathing on my neck.

She whispered in my ear "We're going to be okay."

I laid in bed, almost as if I was paralyzed, unable to move any muscle in my body. Sofia began rubbing my chest with her hand. I hadn't been this close to her in years. It constantly felt like there was some boundary between us, but now there wasn't something in the way.

"I'm going to take care of you."

Sofia kissed me on the chest.

"And we're going to have a beautiful family together."

She reached down and grabbed my hand. She was so intimate it felt like I was dreaming.

"I want to move somewhere quiet where it's just you and me. We could live like we were the last two people on earth."

Sofia kissed me on the lips as I remained silent.

"Would you like that?"

I nodded my head.

Sofia laid her head on my chest. It reminded me of back when we were in high school and she'd sneak through my bedroom window. She'd be angry over her parents most time and she just needed a place where she felt safe. I miss those days. That was back when she felt comfortable with me, when I knew all her secrets and we didn't keep a single thing from each other.

It had been several weeks since my stay in the cabin. Winter was passing and it was beginning to get warmer again. I was now walking with a cane everywhere I went. Without it I'd lose my balance within only a couple of feet. It was just something I would have to get used too.

Sofia and I began packing the house; we were trying to take as little as we could; the rest we would leave behind for the next owners. We were looking for a house with a couple hundred acres of land.

It took us only nine days to find a place way out in the country. The home was on a ranch, although all the cattle and other animals had already been transported somewhere else. The home had five bedrooms, a dining room, and a fairly decent sized kitchen. It was also a lot cheaper than any home you would find in the city. Sofia figured it would be a wonderful place to pick up her photography again and with my disability and VA loans, the house was will in our price range. We took it.

The house was a fixer-upper we soon discovered. The realtor failed to show us its deviancies that the average human eye would miss. It was a work in progress for the both of us. It gave me something productive to do with my time other than sit around all day and wait for night to come.

After we had settled in, Sofia started reconnecting with some of her friends from high school. Every night before we went to bed, she would have side conversations with various friends. She asked me if it would be alright to have some company stay over for some time. The visit would be more than a few days because the drive from California was more than thirty-six hours long.

At the time, I was enjoying our peace and quiet among each other and not having another house within two miles of us. We were living as adults and didn't have the potential drama that the city brings. I could only dodge her question for so long. I eventually gave in and told her it would be fine.

I began clearing out a spare room for Emma and Brad Foster, a couple who had been together since high school. They both went to NYU and graduated with a degree in business. They both had high paying jobs and lived in luxury in the upper class part of Manhattan. I was curious as to see their expressions when they saw our middle class home in the middle of nowhere. However, I wasn't worried about impressing them much either.

This visit seemed out of the ordinary for Sofia, but she insisted she wanted to get back in touch with her old friends. She made a few last minute stops at the store to buy some wine and whiskey.

These days I wasn't drinking much, maybe once every month but no more than that. I was no longer battling my addiction with pills. For the first time in a while, Sofia and I actually had a healthy relationship.

Emma and Brad took a cab from the airport to our home. We offered to come pick them up, but they refused.

It came by surprise when a six year old boy came out of the taxi with them. Sofia never informed me they had any kids or were bringing a kid. This meant I had to situate the house a little more. Thankfully, we had so many bedrooms; it was easy for me to put in a blow up mattress in a room right next to Brad and Emma's.

I shook hands with Brad, who didn't look like he was aging to well, and Sofia gave Emma a rather long hug. I honestly never hung around Brad too much in high school; he played sports and I didn't. The way Sofia described him; he was the perfect husband for Emma.

Brad brought a case of Budweiser beer with him and we stuck it in the fridge. It had been a long time since I had drunk beer; I had always preferred hard alcohol.

Sofia had meat loaf in the oven and was cutting up lettuce for the salad when I came up right behind her.

"You didn't tell me they had a child."

"I know isn't he so cute?"

Sofia obviously missed my point, when I tried to help her cut up the vegetables she shrugged me away.

"Go watch the game honey."

Emma entered the kitchen with an apron on.

"Yeah we've got this. You and Brad go do whatever it is you boys do."

I gave a decent smile and walked into the living room.

In the living room, Brad was playing with his son. He had action figures laid all across the carpet. Brad looked genuinely happy to be a father and to interact with his son. I couldn't help but think that somewhere along the line it had cost him. I saw a man that sacrificed his real ambitions in life. Brad could have played for any college football team he wanted back in his prime, but instead, he was playing with toys. I wondered if it was by choice or if the child was unexpected.

"Brad, you want a beer?"

Brad looked up and nodded his head.

"Sure I'll take a cold one."

I went into the fridge and grabbed of couple beers; I couldn't help but notice Sofia and Emma in the kitchen. She looked so happy to have a conversation with someone else. I thought to myself, "Whose decision was it to live out here, more of mine or hers?" I left the two of them alone and walked back into the living room to watch the game.

The meat loaf came out a little over cooked, but Brad and Emma did their very best to complement Sofia on her cooking. I think somewhere between the several bottles of wine Sofia and Emma had lost track of time. It was strange to see Sofia drinking; it had been since high school, the last time I saw her take a sip of anything.

Brad came out of the kitchen with a bottle of my Johnny Walker that was barely open.

"So you still keep it on top of the refrigerator I see. You mind if we have something a little heavier?"

I was confused as to why he knew where I kept my whiskey. It didn't take long for me to put two and two together and realize Sofia must have said something to them about my problem.

"Why not? Pour me one as well."

Sofia looked at me not knowing whether to be worried or not. She knew it had been awhile since I had agreed to have a drink with anyone. After a moment, she turned around and pretended she didn't see anything.

If she had told Brad and Emma about my drinking, I questioned what else she told them about me. A lot of things had gone on since we decided to get back together. Things I wouldn't want anyone else to know. I wasn't as worried as what they might think of me; I was worried of anything that could damage our relationship. We didn't need anyone else putting in their two cents.

While I poured myself another drink, I sat back at the table and watched Brad and Emma: the way their hands moved, the tones of their voices, how close they sat next to each other at the dinner table. It seemed like every other second he was smiling and she was laughing or vice versa.

I stared down at my plate and looked at the meatloaf; it wasn't cooked how I liked it. It was cold and falling apart, the longer I proceeded to look at it, the sicker I became. The thought alone of biting into it made my stomach turn.

Sofia put her hand on top of mine.

"Are you alright?"

I looked up at her; all conversation began to die down.

"Do you not like it?"

I snapped back into reality and regained my focus.

"It's lovely, babe."

I reached for the Johnny Walker and poured myself another drink; I was already on my fourth one. Sofia seemed concerned every time I took a drink but she was too embarrassed to say anything to me about it.

After dinner, I had stepped outside with Brad to have a cigarette. Sofia and Emma were both washing the dishes together in the kitchen. Brad and I were standing on the front porch I hadn't quite finished building yet. A tiny lamp above us was our only light.

"Sofia tells me you're putting some work into this place.

"Just little things here and there."

I had a drag of my cigarette followed by a sip of my whiskey.

"There's not much to journal about out here."

I sighed and took another drag.

"I gave up on writing a long time ago."

Brad looked out north and watched the wind blow through the trees.

"I guess everyone has to grow up sometime."

Brad took a drag and pointed at the end of the porch.

"The wood is a little uneven over there. Did you lay the foundation yourself?"

I let out a fake laugh.

"I like to have something to keep me busy."

Brad swept the porch with his foot.

"You might want to think about putting a mat down as well. I hear ice is a big issue around these parts."

I was beginning to get fascinated with all the criticism Brad was handing out, especially coming from a man who lives in an apartment.

"So I have to ask the question Ollie . . . how did you convince Sofia to be with you. I'm sorry, I just have to know."

I put my cigarette out on the porch.

"Easy . . . I married her."

I took another drink and walked back inside.

That night, I waited for everyone to go to bed so I could be alone at the kitchen table. I sat up thinking about Brad and Emma's perfect life and how much better it was compared to mine. I had a bottle of Whiskey and Vodka in front of me. I figured it would last me the night. I wasn't afraid of Sofia coming down and seeing me. I bet if she did, she still wouldn't say anything to me. I wouldn't be able to get a reaction out of her even if I tried.

I spotted two bugs on the floor, I watched as one bug ate while the other one got eaten. Which bug was I? Was I the one helplessly being attacked or was I the one suffocating and running out of air to breathe. The room began to feel smaller around me like the walls were caving in on every side. I started to get the spins as well. None of these things could stop me from drinking, not after the night I had.

I heard footsteps coming down the stairs. After a few seconds, the little boy walked into the kitchen. He tapped me on the arm.

"Why aren't you asleep?"

At first, I didn't know what to say. I didn't have any younger siblings growing up. I didn't even know what to talk about to a six year old. What's appropriate and what's not?

"I can't sleep."

The boy walked around the table and climbed on to a chair across from me.

"I can't sleep either."

The boy put his head in the palm of his hands.

"Why don't you play with you action figures or something?"

"Because they're boring."

I took a drink of my whiskey.

"What's so boring about them?"

"They aren't real"

I wiped my face with my hand; I was beginning to get a cold sweat.

"Some things in life aren't real for a reason. You'll figure that out one day when you're older."

"But I already am old."

I let out a depressing laugh.

"Are you going to be like your father when you grow up?

The boy shook his head "no".

"What about your mother?"

The boy once again shook his head "no".

"Well then, who you going to be like?"

The boy pointed his finger at me.

"I want to be like you."

I thought about how bad of a life the boy would have and all the bullshit he would go through if he was to grow up to be like me.

Suddenly, Brad came into the room and saw the boy at the table.

"Hey Buddy, what are you doing out of bed?"

The boy shrugged his shoulders "I don't know."

Brad reached down and picked up his son.

"Come on, let's go back to sleep."

The two of them walked out of the room together, leaving me at table with only a bottle of whiskey. I lit a cigarette and sat back. There was only one bug on the floor now, lying dead.

# Chapter IX

## Death Bed

I often wondered how I would spend the final chapter of my life. It seems like for the past decade I've stayed on the same road of destruction with the wind blowing the same debris in my face. I had built my own home, had hunted for my own food, and had loved and hated the same woman with equal measures. Where was my devotion in the midst of everything going on around me?

I had an epiphany not too long ago, that the light in my life had scared me much more than the dark. Because when everything was brought out in the light, there were no delusions.

Things that would traumatize most people had zero effect on me. There was once a time when the simple mention of a woman's name would strike a never in my body, but not anymore.

It had proved to be too difficult for Sofia and I to fix things, too many ends where falling apart all at once. She had confided in me that she was pregnant once with my child. She told me it was right after high school when she found out about it. Whether or not that was her excuse for breaking things off, I will never know. I think deep down inside, she knew the decision to have an abortion was one that only she could make. Would it have been much uglier if a child was involved, or would that have saved us? Maybe she thought we weren't good enough to be parents, or just that I wasn't good enough to be a father. Could I really blame her?

I was sitting in a plane nineteen-thousand feet in the air flying over the Pacific Ocean. The airline had made a mistake and given me a first class seat. I closed the window blind next to me. I wanted to make it as dark as I could. The flight attendant kept coming by every thirty minutes or so and refilling my little plastic cup with vodka. I think she could tell my trip to California wasn't for business.

I had shaved my face early in the morning, gotten rid of my roguish beard and long hair. I was dressed in a Suit and black dress pants; I was headed to a funeral.

I pulled out a voice recorder from my pocket and put it to my ear. I pressed play over and over again. The voice on the tape was Sofia's.

"I could never leave you."

I could not get her voice out of my head.

Sofia had fallen ill with terminal brain cancer and passed away shortly after. The doctors had given her only a couple weeks but she managed to hold out for three months. I couldn't convince myself to go and see her.

I glanced at the empty seat next to me. Was it a coincidence that no one was assigned there? Are we all just passengers in this world, riding along with someone else steering us along the way?

I was forty one years old at this time. The tale is that we get wiser with age, but how much of that is true? If twenty years ago, someone was to sit next to me on this very same plane, would life have turned out differently? I argue that it wouldn't. Sometimes we don't have the option of who sits next to us, who we converse with, and who we love.

Under all the piles of shit, Sofia was who I was given. The battle I had with depression was all part of the package that came with loving her.

I reached into my other coat pocket and pulled out the picture Sofia had given to me when I was younger. It still hurt to read the letters on the back of it ""I see nothing in them. I simply push the button and take the fucking picture. I don't care for the sights in them or the people in them. They mean nothing to me."

Once the plane landed and I stepped off, I remember feeling this disappointment that it didn't crash in midair. That's when it hit me how corrupt my life had become. I was ready to take responsibility for everyone else's death just so I could be satisfied. I was absolute evil; this wasn't how I was raised.

I sat at a bar inside the airport and continued to drink just like I always had in situations in which I didn't feel comfortable in. I might have been on my twentieth drink, for all I know. I had a good hour to waste until I needed to be on my way. I ordered myself something to eat in the food court, but when it was finally brought to me, I wasn't even hungry.

I pulled out the voice recorder and listened to it again.

"I could never leave you."

It sounded like Sofia was on her death bed when she recorded it. I couldn't help but think how I wouldn't need a voice recorder if I would have been there with her, but it's complicated to explain.

I stood outside the airport by the delta airlines smoking a cigarette. I looked out into the rows of taxis and picked one; ABC cab won the drawl. I shoved my one luggage bag in the trunk and sat in the backseat.

The taxi driver attempted to engage me in a conversation, but I wasn't up to small talk. I realized how drunk I was and thought it'd be a good idea to try and sleep some of it off.

From LAX to Rancho Santa Margarita was about a two hour drive, but with traffic it turned into four, especially since seeing as how the holiday season was approaching.

The driver kept switching radio channels and asking me what kind of music I listened too. I told him anything was fine. He ended up leaving it on some classical music station, which played the likes of "Beethoven", "Bach", and "Dvorak", all composers that reminded me of a history class I had once taken with Sofia. The music seemed to put me to sleep rather quickly.

I arrived in Ranch Santa Margarita around 4 P.M. I had the driver drop me off at an old café built back in the seventies. I paid him an enormous fee and grabbed my luggage from the trunk.

While sitting inside the café drinking black coffee and trying to sober up, I contemplated calling up my folks and telling them I was in town. After a few minutes I decided I would regret the decision if I did. The fewer people that knew I was in town, the better.

The funeral took place in the catholic memorial. Sofia never expressed to me where she wanted to be buried, but her parents already had a family plot.

I kept my distance from the rest of the crowd; the majority of the people present were Sofia's immediate and extended family. Some of the people we went to high school with were also there. Most of them were married with two or three kids.

Mickey Childs walked up to me with a cigarette in his hand. I couldn't help but think of the irony that we actually ran into each other again and that he was still living in the same area.

"Are you coming to the home afterwards?"

"I don't know if that's such a brilliant idea."

Mickey took a drag of his cigarette.

"We're all as guilty as you. Every one of us fell by the way side when it came to Sofia."

I couldn't agree with Mickey. I could dissect the circumstance from every angle and I'd still come up with the same value. For some reason, I reluctantly decided to follow Mickey to her parents' home.

It felt like déjà vu e entering the home, but I still felt out of place with the rest of the people surrounding me.

I walked into the kitchen to pour myself some water when I saw Sofia's father, Herald, sitting at the bar counter. There was a bottle of booze with the cap off right in front of him. From the looks of the dazed expression on his face, I could sense he had started drinking as soon as he got home.

Herald looked up at me.

"Want to take a seat?"

Herald pulled out a chair right beside him.

Against my instincts, I sat down.

"Have a drink."

Before I could say anything, Herald had already started pouring me a glass of whiskey. He slid it over to me carelessly.

"I couldn't believe she was forty-one. My best memories of her were when she was barely as tall as that chair you're sitting in."

Herald looked at me with confusion in his eyes.

"What was she like?"

Before I could answer, Herald interrupted.

"Jesus I'm asking someone else what my own daughter was like. How pathetic is that?"

Herald poured himself a few inches of whiskey.

"She was beautiful."

I wasn't lying to Herald. Sofia was absolutely beautiful. Through all our years together I don't remember telling her that once. There were a lot of things I wish I would have told her. All those mornings I wasted, ignoring her while she stood there and took care of me. All those nights I stayed up drinking instead of going to bed with her and making love.

Herald turned and leaned in towards me.

"She loved you, that was about the only thing I knew about her. She would go on and on about you every time I'd call her."

I watched as Herald's hands shook while he tried holding up his glass.

"All I ever wanted for her was to find a man that wasn't anything like her father. The way I treated her mother was so horrible. I let her think that type of behavior was acceptable. I had no idea how to raise a child and she was the first born.

"I think we all have times in our lives when we have no fucking idea what we're doing."

I finished my drink and stood up from the bar counter.

I decided to walk upstairs and go into Sofia's old bedroom. It looked like the average teen room with posters all over the wall of her favorite bands.

Near the window she had a collage of photos she had taken throughout her high school years. The first couple rows of photo were all nature, with pictures of valleys, the shy, and highways. Sofia had a very modern taste.

At the very bottom of the collage for a mere second I thought there was a photo of Sofia and me, but as I looked closer I realized it was Sofia with somebody else.

On her bookshelves she still had stacks of scripts and stories that I had given to her from my journalism classes. I had thrown away all the original copies I had years ago. Beside the collage and the scripts, there was one more thing that stood out to me. In the very corner of her room there was a canvas with a variety of colors splashed across it. I remembered seeing the painting years ago in her apartment.

"Mind if I come in?"

I turned around to see Mickey Childs standing in the doorway.

"Sure."

I hadn't seen Mickey in what felt like an eternity. Much like Brad, the years had definitely taken its toll on him. He had a large stomach and a small patch of hair left on his head.

Mickey made his way next to the corner with me.

"How are you handling things?"

I thought long and hard how to answer Mickey's question.

"I'll tell you when I know."

Mickey looked out the window. There wasn't a cloud in the sky and the sun was getting ready to go down.

"I knew how much you loved her Ollie."

I looked away from the painting and faced Mickey.

"No, you really don't.

I reached down and picked up the painting. It was time to leave.

I took the red eye flight back to New England. The cabin was mostly empty. This time I sat in the very back. I opened up the window blind to see the dark sky. The flight attendant came by and asked if I wanted a drink. To my surprise, I told her no.

I pulled out the voice recorder once more and played it again. The sound of Sofia's voice was the only thing I ever wanted to hear anymore.

"I could never leave you."

# Chapter X

## Silent Film

It had been a year since Sofia's death and I was forty-three years old now. The date was August 1, 2015. The weather forecast was predicting a hurricane would be coming through this month. The area I was living in hadn't seen weather like this since the nineties.

The hurricane didn't alarm me any. I assumed it would pass right by us and that life would keep going. However, the towns people made mention of a mandatory evacuation if conditions were to get any worse.

I made the decision since the rumors first started that I wasn't going anywhere. I would hold down the fort regardless of what everyone else did. This was my home and I wasn't abandoning it.

I woke up in the middle of the night on August 10th. Something smelt like it was burning in the bedroom. I got out of bed and walked around the room trying to find from where the smell was coming. The further I got away from the bed, the less I could smell it.

I grabbed a flashlight off of the nightstand and looked under the bed, but nothing was there. When I came back up, I put the light on the sheets. I could see little tiny dots on the side of the bed where Sofia used to sleep. I moved closer and slowly pulled the covers off. That's when I saw a black mold covering the bottom of the mattress. I quickly stood up and turned the light on.

This was the first time I had ever seen mold in the house. I couldn't understand how it was possible that it was growing on the bed. I went downstairs and slept on the couch. I decided I would do something about it the next day.

I woke up around 8 a.m. When I went back into the bedroom to take a second look at the mattress, I saw that the black mold had spread even more.

There was never any mention of black mold when I bought the house from the real estate company, nor did the previous owners disclose any information that it was there. Somehow it had managed to also slip by the house inspection.

I decided to take the bed out in the backyard and burn it. While I did so, I made sure to wear a face mask so I wouldn't inhale the fumes. I would crash on the couch until I was able to get someone out here to look for anymore mold growing in the house.

The phones lines were down due to the heavy winds, so there was no getting ahold of the Real Estate agency. I went into the kitchen and made myself a cup of coffee. I could hear the wind blowing the branches against the side of the house.

Out of the corner of my eye I spotted black spots on the counter that looked like fingerprints. I wet a paper towel and tried to wash it off. No matter how hard I wiped, the fingerprints would not go away. I tried to think what I had touched to leave such a stain. Maybe it was from burning the mattress.

While I was in the kitchen sipping on my coffee, I couldn't help but feel on edge. I was having strange thoughts that reminded me of when I used to drink heavily. I went into the bathroom and took an aspirin; maybe if I laid down, I would feel a little better.

A few hours had passed by and I woke up in a cold sweat with the television playing. Some paid programming show was repeating over and over. I sat up and put both feet on the floor. My head felt like it was ready to explode. I felt something falling on the back of my neck; I looked up to see what seemed like ashes coming from the ceiling. Not only that, but the same fingerprints I saw on the counter earlier that day, were now on the ceiling. And I couldn't help but feeling like someone was watching me.

Something must be going on in the upstairs bedroom. I walked up the staircase, which seemed to be creaking more than usual. When I opened the door to the master bedroom, I saw the hardwood floor beginning to rot. I moved towards it to get a better look.

Suddenly I heard the sound of someone whistling. It was coming from behind the bathroom door. Black fingerprints were smeared all around the door knob. I put my hand on the doorknob and turned it. When I did this, the whistling stopped.

I pushed the door open slowly. Standing in the bathroom was Sofia combing her hair. She turned around and smiled at me. This clearly had to be a figment of my imagination. I had just gotten back from her funeral.

"You want to watch a movie tonight?"

Every muscle in my body was completely frozen. How should someone react in this situation?

"I'll meet you downstairs in a couple of minutes. I'm almost done."

I took a step back. I must be losing my mind. People just don't come back from the dead.

As crazy as it seemed, I went downstairs and sat on the couch. I put an old black and white silent film in the DVD player. Was I actually waiting for her to come downstairs? It wasn't healthy of me to pretend like this. It's only a game inside my mind.

I felt fingernails on the back of my neck, then hands running up my shoulder blades. Sofia came around from behind the couch and straddled herself on top of me. She reached up and flicked the switch on the lamp turning the light off.

"Things are the way I've always wanted them to be . . . . just you and me."

Sofia took her night gown off; she grabbed both of my hands and put them on her naked body. She leaned in and kissed me on the lips. That night I made love to a ghost.

I figured in the morning, I would wake up and it would all just be a dream my mind had used to play an evil trick on me. I went into the kitchen to put on another cup of coffee and that's when I saw Sofia making me breakfast.

"Eggs and bacon, right?"

From that point on, I decided that no matter how crazy it sounded I would go along with whatever chemical unbalance was causing this reaction in my brain.

As the weeks progressed, I began to fall back in love with Sofia. I was being given a second chance to make right with her. I never left the house; I would stay in bed with her all day. I kept all the curtains in the house closed and got by with as little light as possible.

In spite of everything that seemed to be going well, I began to notice that Sofia was dropping weight incredibly fast. It only took me one arm to wrap around her. Whenever she cooked, she wouldn't eat anything. She always told me she wasn't hungry.

On August 16, Sofia put on a black dress she had purchased years ago. She asked me if I would dance with her. She pulled out an old classical record of symphonies and put it in the player. When I watched her put the needle on the record, I could tell that her fingernails were all black underneath. Not only that, but she was much paler than before.

The two of us danced together as the night progressed. We both fell asleep lying naked on each other in the living room.

In the middle of the night, I woke up and lit myself a cigarette. I could hear the wind blowing hard outside the house. For the first time in weeks, I took a step out. The grass smelt like the scent of rain. The hurricane had not yet passed, but news reports kept battling back and forth between calling it a hurricane or a tropical storm. I still believed it wouldn't touch this side of the state.

I sat down on a wooden chair and tried processing all that was happening. I never thought there was such thing as life after death, which had to mean that Sofia had never really died. So, was the plane ride all a dream? Was the funeral completely made up?

I had with me the voice recorder. I listened to it over and over so often that I had believed they were Sofia's last words. I pressed played. Seconds passed on and there was nothing but white noise.

I rewound the voice recorder once more and listened to it over again, but still there was only white noise.

"Come inside."

I turned around to see Sofia standing behind the door with her gown on.

"It's cold, you could get sick."

I took another drag of my cigarette and exhaled; I put the cigarette out in the ashtray and followed Sofia back inside.

The next morning, I was watching the news with Sofia when an emergency alert came on the television. The hurricane was headed in our direction and it was estimated to hit full force by 2 A.M. the following day. I turned to Sofia and asked her what she wanted to do.

She told me that if we left, the two us could no longer be together and that she would disappear. I promised her that wouldn't happen. I took a final trip to the hardware store and bought a large amount of lumber, nails, and an assortment of construction tools.

I spent the daylight hours boarding up all the windows and cracks with big wood panels but, as I soon discovered the black mold had spread rapidly. I made best with what I could and hoped that it would hold. All that was left to do was to wait.

Around midnight, Sofia and I sat together hand in hand on the couch. The power was already out and the house began to shake. She leaned over and whispered in my ear.

"I love you."

I kissed her on the side of her cheek.

"I love you too."

The trees broke straight through the windows and ripped the wood panels in shreds. And as the water came rushing into the house, I assured Sofia that we would always be together and that this was our own little home.

# Epilogue

Sofia and I were dead.

I was living in a state of delirium. I saw a thousand colors flash before my eyes; I was completely delusional to my surroundings. The ocean had taken its new territory and there was no more dry land.

I looked up above me; the sky was covered with a blanket of blackness. The wind brushed against my skin and I could feel its unforgiving coldness. A thousand senses struck through my nerves. My body was in an utter shock.

The ocean was so clean and clear I could see my reflection in it. I was only skin and bones with not an inch of meat on me. Underneath my fingernails was the soil from the earth. I bent down and began coughing up water.

I saw Sofia standing in front of me, drenched wet in her black dress. Her long hair hung down to her elbows. She slowly stepped closer to me. I reached out my hand to her. She grasped my hand and held it tight.

I could feel my heart beating through my chest like it was ready to explode. Sofia kneeled down in the water in front of me. She kissed me on top of my head. The ground began to shake the earth, I looked out as far as my eyes would allow. The waves were rising straight through the air and then falling back down.

I began to hallucinate fragments of my past life, I remembered being passed out on the couch watching the old DVD of me and

Sofia, that night I had easily taken enough pills to successfully kill myself.

I saw the Navy Vessel a couple hundred yards out cruising through the storm. I was standing on the railing of the ship when I slipped and caught my leg in the rope. Except for this time I wasn't rescued by the crew members, and thus I drowned in the water. Afterwards they had followed out my wishes and buried me at sea, the true home to any seamen.

The winter I had spent out in the Northern Mountains. How I was stranded all alone in the cold. And how I had shot that deer and left it bleeding to death in the snow. I wondered how long it took that deer to finally die. I had no memory of someone taking me to the hospital. Did I accept defeat out in the mountains?

The plane I was flying in nineteen-thousand feet in the air. A few seconds after receiving my first drink, the plane had engine failure and crashed into a field, killing all a hundred and seventy-five passengers.

Finally the hurricane that flew over our house; the ocean had washed away our home and everything in it. I could still feel the water in my lungs.

I was proof that we live again. It's not the afterlife though. The earth itself had shifted, rotated its axes, and became something else entirely.

Sofia and I stood, watching the universe change. The both of us were high together. I whispered in her ear, the same words she had said to me so many times before.

"I could never leave you."

*An excerpt from William L.G. Stephens's next novella:* **Twelve Leaves**

# Chapter I

## Through Hell and High Water

As I walked through the Suicide Forest, I saw many familiar people that use to be alive. Though their faces had become decayed and smelt of rotten flesh. I could still hear the sound of their souls flying through the infected air that poisoned their lungs. Once their bodies were torn apart, their limbs became attached to the roots and grew on to the trees. Their eyes were to be forever opened, so they could watch the rest of the dead using their arms and legs.

It was my job to bring the bodies of suicide to the giant tree that raised higher than the earth's tallest building. The first body to be placed on the tree was Benjamin Alazet, back in the sixteenth century. Although Benjamin was not the first person to commit suicide he was the first name written in the suicide log. Lucifer had chosen him to be a symbol of what was his most hellacious realm.

I carried around the suicide log at all times. It was my duty to fill the lines with countless names of the dead. I had entered Hell seventy five years ago after hanging myself from a rope in my barn house. One thing I could never find out was who had my job before me. Nowhere in the suicide log was it mentioned the names of who have formerly held my position.

There must have been a particular reason for their absences in the log. I was only told a certain number of instructions at a time from Lucifer; he didn't trust anyone with information that could be leaked to the other demons. In return for my duties I was given, Lucifer let me keep my human figure. Unlike all the others, who had their eyes removed, or half of their face scarred from being shoved into the belly of fires.

I made numerous trips to the other thirteen reams of hell, where the whores were condemned to being raped over and over for all eternity. The realm below the whores was where the murders were at; they were punished before they even entered the gates of hell. Jesus Christ himself had tortured the murders with several of his own techniques, when they finally became the possession of Lucifer. He chose to instead give them the royal treatment.

At the very first realm was where the drug dealers lived, their duty was to keep producing whichever drug was their specialty and pass it on to the realms below them. I was constantly shooting up heroin into my veins and snorting cocaine through my nostrils.

The drugs took away my senses, which saved me from smelling burning flesh constantly. In hell there is no track of time, there is no night or day. Colors of red and black are the only colors found. The flames spread through hell like a wildfire, but most notably in the belly of hell, which was at the very bottom.

The belly is where the Host stood, with his black suit and top hat. The Host introduced all the new arrivals to their new home. He filled their minds with thoughts of evil and torment, he got off on their cries and there pleading for Jesus to except them into the gates of heaven. Jesus could hear every last one of their words, just like he heard everything else that made sound, but never once did he reply back.

Once you died and became the possession of Lucifer, there is no going back, Jesus will not forgive you, and Lucifer well not feel the least bit of pity for you. It didn't make a difference whether you accepted your final destination or not, it would be where you would spend eternity.

Quite often I would write names into the logs of souls that Jesus had sent down to Hell. The souls he didn't believe lived up to the standard that he expected them too. Depending on his decision he would either send them back to earth or to us, no matter what however they would eventually arrive in the belly.

Hell is the oldest form of a business. Just as companies on earth and the stock market, there was evidence of corruption all around. People fucking other people over was a trait that Lucifer himself had planted inside the living's mind, much like a worm that crawled through their system leaving eggs inside their blood cells.

Once you entered Hell, you could visibly see the worms crawling through your skin, periodically they would swim in the back of your throat causing you to vomit them up. The worms burned like acid on Hell's ground. There was in infinity supply of these worms, for they were Lucifer's own pets.


I made my rounds to the belly of Hell, and came upon fifty suicides in the last ten minutes. I called for my slaves who were built like gladiators. They began dragging the bodies to the Suicide forest like I told them to do. I reached down and grabbed the legs of the smallest body. It was a teenage girl, no older than sixteen. She had slit her wrists and bled out in the bathroom while both her parents were at work.

Once I made it to the Suicide forest, my slaves came up to me and gave me the names of the newcomers. I jotted them all down in my log. Pretty soon I would need another log book. I was already on Volume One hundred and ten. Each log book consisted of three thousand pages. Each page could hold twenty nine names. Beside their names I would write down their birthdate and the day they died. This was the only occasion that time was used in the underworld.

I felt no pity putting the bodies next to the tree and letting the roots attach to their limbs and make whole with them. No one in Hell feels pity for anyone. It's exactly the opposite. In Hell misery loves company.

I finished writing down the fifty names, and dragging their bodies to the forest. I stood back and watched as the roots quickly grew into their bones. Their eyes opened up in horror to what was being done to them. One by one their limbs were ripped apart and taken away from them.